Don't Rock the Boat

A Boating Logbook with Safety Checklists, Trip Logs, Journal Pages, Maintenance Record-Keeping, and Important Reference Information

Captain Jack

Introduction

Hello and congratulations on purchasing Don't Rock the Boat!

Inside, you will find boating information along with many pages to journal your trips and boat maintenance.

Using this book on each of your trips with family and friends will help you keep track of all your boating activities.

The journaling can be for your memories and also used to log hours if you would someday like to get a US Coast Guard Boat Captain's License.

Without further ado, let's get started!

Force	Wind Knots	
0	Less than 1	
1	1-3	Calm
2	4-6	Light Air
3	7-10	Light Breeze
4	11-16	Gentle Breeze
5	17-21	Moderate Breeze
6	22-27	Fresh Breeze
7	28-33	Strong Breeze
8	34-40	Near Gale
9	41-47	Gale
10	48-55	Strong Gale
11	56-63	Storm
12	64	Violent Storm

Speed
Conversions

Knots	MPH	K/PH
5	5.8	2.7
10	11.5	5.4
15	17.3	8.1
20	23.0	10.8
25	28.8	13.5
30	34.5	16.2
35	40.3	18.9
40	46.0	21.6
45	51.8	24.3
50	57.5	27.0
55	63.3	29.7
60	69.0	32.4
65	74.8	35.1
70	80.6	37.8
75	86.3	40.5
80	92.1	43.2
85	97.8	45.9
90	103.6	48.6
95	109.3	51.3
100	115.1	54.0

BOAT EQUIPMENT CHECKLIST

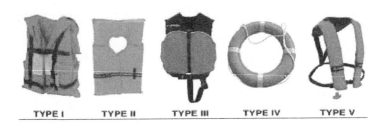

TYPE I   TYPE II   TYPE III   TYPE IV   TYPE V

___ Personal Floatation Devices
One Type I, II, or III for each
Person on board.

___ Toolbox and Tools
Tools necessary for basic
repairs.

___ First Aid Kit
Know how to use all
supplies in the kit.

___ Throwable Floatation
A Type IV device

___ Registration/Licenses,
Decals, Permits & Insurance

___ Fuel, Oil, Lights,
Horn & Batteries Check

___ VHF Radio

___ Cell Phone & Charger

___ GPS Locater

___ Boat Hook and Mooring
Lines

___ Anchor & Anchor line
approved for depth

___ Fire Extinguisher
Boat Class determines type

___ Drinking Water

___ Sun Protection

___ Binoculars

Vessel Statistics

Vessel Name _____

Make _____	Type _____
Model _____	Hull ID # _____
Year _____	Registration # _____
Color _____	
Length Overall _____	Dry Weight _____
Beam _____	Bridge Clearance _____

Capacities (Gal.)	**Generator**
Fresh Water _____	Make _____
Black Water _____	Serial Number _____
Grey Water _____	Oil Capacity _____
Fuel _____	Coolant Capacity _____
	Oil Filter _____
	Fuel Filter _____
	Water Seperator Filter _____

Engine #1	**Engine #2**
Make _____	Make _____
Serial Number _____	Serial Number _____
Oil Capacity _____	Oil Capacity _____
Coolant Capacity _____	Coolant Capacity _____
Oil Filter _____	Oil Filter _____
Fuel Filter _____	Fuel Filter _____
Water Seperator Filter _____	Water Seperator Filter _____

Battery #1	**Battery #2**
Manufacturer _____	Manufacturer _____
Type _____	Type _____
Part Number _____	Part Number _____

Battery #3	**Battery #4**
Manufacturer _____	Manufacturer _____
Type _____	Type _____
Part Number _____	Part Number _____

Notes

Now the earth was formless and empty, darkness covered the surface of the watery depths, and the Spirit of God was hovering over the surface of the waters. Genesis 1:2

Trip Log

Vessel Name _____

Body of Water _____

Month _____ Official Number _____

Year _____ Gross Tonnage _____

Days Underway _____ Weather _____

Position Served _____ Fuel _____

Master Name _____

Notes _____

_____

_____

_____

_____

Vessel Name _____

Body of Water _____

Month _____ Official Number _____

Year _____ Gross Tonnage _____

Days Underway _____ Weather _____

Position Served _____ Fuel _____

Master Name _____

Notes _____

_____

_____

_____

_____

Trip Log

Vessel Name _____

Body of Water _____

Month _____ Official Number _____

Year _____ Gross Tonnage _____

Days Underway _____ Weather _____

Position Served _____ Fuel _____

Master Name _____

Notes _____

_____

_____

_____

_____

Vessel Name _____

Body of Water _____

Month _____ Official Number _____

Year _____ Gross Tonnage _____

Days Underway _____ Weather _____

Position Served _____ Fuel _____

Master Name _____

Notes _____

_____

_____

_____

Trip Log

Vessel Name _____

Body of Water _____

Month _____ Official Number _____

Year _____ Gross Tonnage _____

Days Underway _____ Weather _____

Position Served _____ Fuel _____

Master Name _____

Notes _____

_____

_____

_____

_____

Vessel Name _____

Body of Water _____

Month _____ Official Number _____

Year _____ Gross Tonnage _____

Days Underway _____ Weather _____

Position Served _____ Fuel _____

Master Name _____

Notes _____

_____

_____

_____

_____

Trip Log

Vessel Name _____

Body of Water _____

Month _____ Official Number _____

Year _____ Gross Tonnage _____

Days Underway _____ Weather _____

Position Served _____ Fuel _____

Master Name _____

Notes _____

_____

_____

_____

_____

Vessel Name _____

Body of Water _____

Month _____ Official Number _____

Year _____ Gross Tonnage _____

Days Underway _____ Weather _____

Position Served _____ Fuel _____

Master Name _____

Notes _____

_____

_____

_____

_____

Trip Log

Vessel Name _____

Body of Water _____

Month _____ Official Number _____

Year _____ Gross Tonnage _____

Days Underway _____ Weather _____

Position Served _____ Fuel _____

Master Name _____

Notes _____

_____

_____

_____

_____

Vessel Name _____

Body of Water _____

Month _____ Official Number _____

Year _____ Gross Tonnage _____

Days Underway _____ Weather _____

Position Served _____ Fuel _____

Master Name _____

Notes _____

_____

_____

_____

_____

Trip Log

Vessel Name _____

Body of Water _____

Month _____   Official Number _____

Year _____   Gross Tonnage _____

Days Underway _____   Weather _____

Position Served _____   Fuel _____

Master Name _____

Notes _____

_____

_____

_____

_____

Vessel Name _____

Body of Water _____

Month _____   Official Number _____

Year _____   Gross Tonnage _____

Days Underway _____   Weather _____

Position Served _____   Fuel _____

Master Name _____

Notes _____

_____

_____

_____

_____

Trip Log

Vessel Name _____
Body of Water _____
Month _____ Official Number _____
Year _____ Gross Tonnage _____
Days Underway _____ Weather _____
Position Served _____ Fuel _____
Master Name _____

Notes _____
_____
_____
_____
_____

Vessel Name _____
Body of Water _____
Month _____ Official Number _____
Year _____ Gross Tonnage _____
Days Underway _____ Weather _____
Position Served _____ Fuel _____
Master Name _____

Notes _____
_____
_____
_____

Trip Log

Vessel Name _____

Body of Water _____

Month _____ Official Number _____

Year _____ Gross Tonnage _____

Days Underway _____ Weather _____

Position Served _____ Fuel _____

Master Name _____

Notes _____
_____
_____
_____
_____

Vessel Name _____

Body of Water _____

Month _____ Official Number _____

Year _____ Gross Tonnage _____

Days Underway _____ Weather _____

Position Served _____ Fuel _____

Master Name _____

Notes _____
_____
_____
_____

Trip Log

Vessel Name _____

Body of Water _____

Month _____ Official Number _____

Year _____ Gross Tonnage _____

Days Underway _____ Weather _____

Position Served _____ Fuel _____

Master Name _____

Notes

_____

_____

_____

_____

_____

Vessel Name _____

Body of Water _____

Month _____ Official Number _____

Year _____ Gross Tonnage _____

Days Underway _____ Weather _____

Position Served _____ Fuel _____

Master Name _____

Notes

_____

_____

_____

_____

Trip Log

Vessel Name _____

Body of Water _____

Month _____ Official Number _____

Year _____ Gross Tonnage _____

Days Underway _____ Weather _____

Position Served _____ Fuel _____

Master Name _____

Notes _____

_____

_____

_____

_____

Vessel Name _____

Body of Water _____

Month _____ Official Number _____

Year _____ Gross Tonnage _____

Days Underway _____ Weather _____

Position Served _____ Fuel _____

Master Name _____

Notes _____

_____

_____

_____

_____

Journal

He alone spreads out the heavens, and treads on the waves of the sea.
Job 9:8

Trip Log

Vessel Name _____

Body of Water _____

Month _____ Official Number _____

Year _____ Gross Tonnage _____

Days Underway _____ Weather _____

Position Served _____ Fuel _____

Master Name _____

Notes _____

_____

_____

_____

_____

Vessel Name _____

Body of Water _____

Month _____ Official Number _____

Year _____ Gross Tonnage _____

Days Underway _____ Weather _____

Position Served _____ Fuel _____

Master Name _____

Notes _____

_____

_____

_____

Trip Log

Vessel Name _____

Body of Water _____

Month _____ Official Number _____

Year _____ Gross Tonnage _____

Days Underway _____ Weather _____

Position Served _____ Fuel _____

Master Name _____

Notes _____

_____

_____

_____

_____

Vessel Name _____

Body of Water _____

Month _____ Official Number _____

Year _____ Gross Tonnage _____

Days Underway _____ Weather _____

Position Served _____ Fuel _____

Master Name _____

Notes _____

_____

_____

_____

_____

Trip Log

Vessel Name _____

Body of Water _____

Month _____ Official Number _____

Year _____ Gross Tonnage _____

Days Underway _____ Weather _____

Position Served _____ Fuel _____

Master Name _____

Notes _____

_____

_____

_____

_____

Vessel Name _____

Body of Water _____

Month _____ Official Number _____

Year _____ Gross Tonnage _____

Days Underway _____ Weather _____

Position Served _____ Fuel _____

Master Name _____

Notes _____

_____

_____

_____

_____

Trip Log

Vessel Name _____

Body of Water _____

Month _____ Official Number _____

Year _____ Gross Tonnage _____

Days Underway _____ Weather _____

Position Served _____ Fuel _____

Master Name _____

Notes _____

_____

_____

_____

_____

_____

Vessel Name _____

Body of Water _____

Month _____ Official Number _____

Year _____ Gross Tonnage _____

Days Underway _____ Weather _____

Position Served _____ Fuel _____

Master Name _____

Notes _____

_____

_____

_____

_____

Trip Log

Vessel Name _____

Body of Water _____

Month _____ Official Number _____

Year _____ Gross Tonnage _____

Days Underway _____ Weather _____

Position Served _____ Fuel _____

Master Name _____

Notes _____

_____

_____

_____

_____

Vessel Name _____

Body of Water _____

Month _____ Official Number _____

Year _____ Gross Tonnage _____

Days Underway _____ Weather _____

Position Served _____ Fuel _____

Master Name _____

Notes _____

_____

_____

_____

_____

Trip Log

Vessel Name _____

Body of Water _____

Month _____ Official Number _____

Year _____ Gross Tonnage _____

Days Underway _____ Weather _____

Position Served _____ Fuel _____

Master Name _____

Notes _____

_____

_____

_____

_____

Vessel Name _____

Body of Water _____

Month _____ Official Number _____

Year _____ Gross Tonnage _____

Days Underway _____ Weather _____

Position Served _____ Fuel _____

Master Name _____

Notes _____

_____

_____

_____

_____

Trip Log

Vessel Name _____

Body of Water _____

Month _____ Official Number _____

Year _____ Gross Tonnage _____

Days Underway _____ Weather _____

Position Served _____ Fuel _____

Master Name _____

Notes _____

_____

_____

_____

_____

Vessel Name _____

Body of Water _____

Month _____ Official Number _____

Year _____ Gross Tonnage _____

Days Underway _____ Weather _____

Position Served _____ Fuel _____

Master Name _____

Notes _____

_____

_____

_____

_____

Trip Log

Vessel Name _____

Body of Water _____

Month _____ Official Number _____

Year _____ Gross Tonnage _____

Days Underway _____ Weather _____

Position Served _____ Fuel _____

Master Name _____

Notes _____

_____

_____

_____

_____

Vessel Name _____

Body of Water _____

Month _____ Official Number _____

Year _____ Gross Tonnage _____

Days Underway _____ Weather _____

Position Served _____ Fuel _____

Master Name _____

Notes _____

_____

_____

_____

_____

Trip Log

Vessel Name _____

Body of Water _____

Month _____ Official Number _____

Year _____ Gross Tonnage _____

Days Underway _____ Weather _____

Position Served _____ Fuel _____

Master Name _____

Notes _____

_____

_____

_____

_____

Vessel Name _____

Body of Water _____

Month _____ Official Number _____

Year _____ Gross Tonnage _____

Days Underway _____ Weather _____

Position Served _____ Fuel _____

Master Name _____

Notes _____

_____

_____

_____

_____

Trip Log

Vessel Name _____

Body of Water _____

Month _____ Official Number _____

Year _____ Gross Tonnage _____

Days Underway _____ Weather _____

Position Served _____ Fuel _____

Master Name _____

Notes _____

_____

_____

_____

_____

Vessel Name _____

Body of Water _____

Month _____ Official Number _____

Year _____ Gross Tonnage _____

Days Underway _____ Weather _____

Position Served _____ Fuel _____

Master Name _____

Notes _____

_____

_____

_____

_____

Journal

He reached down from heaven and took hold of me; He drew me out of deep waters. 2 Samuel 22:17

Trip Log

Vessel Name _____

Body of Water _____

Month _____ Official Number _____

Year _____ Gross Tonnage _____

Days Underway _____ Weather _____

Position Served _____ Fuel _____

Master Name _____

Notes _____

_____

_____

_____

_____

Vessel Name _____

Body of Water _____

Month _____ Official Number _____

Year _____ Gross Tonnage _____

Days Underway _____ Weather _____

Position Served _____ Fuel _____

Master Name _____

Notes _____

_____

_____

_____

_____

Trip Log

Vessel Name _____

Body of Water _____

Month _____   Official Number _____

Year _____   Gross Tonnage _____

Days Underway _____   Weather _____

Position Served _____   Fuel _____

Master Name _____

Notes _____

_____

_____

_____

_____

Vessel Name _____

Body of Water _____

Month _____   Official Number _____

Year _____   Gross Tonnage _____

Days Underway _____   Weather _____

Position Served _____   Fuel _____

Master Name _____

Notes _____

_____

_____

_____

_____

Trip Log

Vessel Name _____

Body of Water _____

Month _____ Official Number _____

Year _____ Gross Tonnage _____

Days Underway _____ Weather _____

Position Served _____ Fuel _____

Master Name _____

Notes _____

_____

_____

_____

_____

Vessel Name _____

Body of Water _____

Month _____ Official Number _____

• Year _____ Gross Tonnage _____

Days Underway _____ Weather _____

Position Served _____ Fuel _____

Master Name _____

Notes _____

_____

_____

_____

_____

Trip Log

Vessel Name _____

Body of Water _____

Month _____ Official Number _____

Year _____ Gross Tonnage _____

Days Underway _____ Weather _____

Position Served _____ Fuel _____

Master Name _____

Notes _____

_____

_____

_____

_____

Vessel Name _____

Body of Water _____

Month _____ Official Number _____

Year _____ Gross Tonnage _____

Days Underway _____ Weather _____

Position Served _____ Fuel _____

Master Name _____

Notes _____

_____

_____

_____

Trip Log

Vessel Name _____

Body of Water _____

Month _____ Official Number _____

Year _____ Gross Tonnage _____

Days Underway _____ Weather _____

Position Served _____ Fuel _____

Master Name _____

Notes _____

_____

_____

_____

_____

Vessel Name _____

Body of Water _____

Month _____ Official Number _____

Year _____ Gross Tonnage _____

Days Underway _____ Weather _____

Position Served _____ Fuel _____

Master Name _____

Notes _____

_____

_____

_____

_____

Trip Log

Vessel Name _____

Body of Water _____

Month _____   Official Number _____

Year _____   Gross Tonnage _____

Days Underway _____   Weather _____

Position Served _____   Fuel _____

Master Name _____

Notes _____

_____

_____

_____

_____

Vessel Name _____

Body of Water _____

Month _____   Official Number _____

Year _____   Gross Tonnage _____

Days Underway _____   Weather _____

Position Served _____   Fuel _____

Master Name _____

Notes _____

_____

_____

_____

_____

Trip Log

Vessel Name _____

Body of Water _____

Month _____ Official Number _____

Year _____ Gross Tonnage _____

Days Underway _____ Weather _____

Position Served _____ Fuel _____

Master Name _____

Notes _____

_____

_____

_____

_____

Vessel Name _____

Body of Water _____

Month _____ Official Number _____

Year _____ Gross Tonnage _____

Days Underway _____ Weather _____

Position Served _____ Fuel _____

Master Name _____

Notes _____

_____

_____

_____

_____

Trip Log

Vessel Name _____

Body of Water _____

Month _____ Official Number _____

Year _____ Gross Tonnage _____

Days Underway _____ Weather _____

Position Served _____ Fuel _____

Master Name _____

Notes

_____

_____

_____

_____

_____

Vessel Name _____

Body of Water _____

Month _____ Official Number _____

Year _____ Gross Tonnage _____

Days Underway _____ Weather _____

Position Served _____ Fuel _____

Master Name _____

Notes

_____

_____

_____

_____

_____

Trip Log

Vessel Name _____

Body of Water _____

Month _____ Official Number _____

Year _____ Gross Tonnage _____

Days Underway _____ Weather _____

Position Served _____ Fuel _____

Master Name _____

Notes _____

_____

_____

_____

_____

Vessel Name _____

Body of Water _____

Month _____ Official Number _____

Year _____ Gross Tonnage _____

Days Underway _____ Weather _____

Position Served _____ Fuel _____

Master Name _____

Notes _____

_____

_____

_____

_____

Trip Log

Vessel Name _____

Body of Water _____

Month _____ Official Number _____

Year _____ Gross Tonnage _____

Days Underway _____ Weather _____

Position Served _____ Fuel _____

Master Name _____

Notes _____

_____

_____

_____

_____

Vessel Name _____

Body of Water _____

Month _____ Official Number _____

Year _____ Gross Tonnage _____

Days Underway _____ Weather _____

Position Served _____ Fuel _____

Master Name _____

Notes _____

_____

_____

_____

Journal

_____
_____
_____
_____
_____
_____
_____
_____
_____
_____
_____
_____
_____
_____
_____
_____
_____
_____
_____
_____
_____
_____
_____
_____
_____
_____

You rule the raging sea; when its waves surge, you still them.
Psalm 89:9

Trip Log

Vessel Name _____

Body of Water _____

Month _____ Official Number _____

Year _____ Gross Tonnage _____

Days Underway _____ Weather _____

Position Served _____ Fuel _____

Master Name _____

Notes _____

_____

_____

_____

_____

Vessel Name _____

Body of Water _____

Month _____ Official Number _____

Year _____ Gross Tonnage _____

Days Underway _____ Weather _____

Position Served _____ Fuel _____

Master Name _____

Notes _____

_____

_____

_____

_____

Trip Log

Vessel Name _____

Body of Water _____

Month _____ Official Number _____

Year _____ Gross Tonnage _____

Days Underway _____ Weather _____

Position Served _____ Fuel _____

Master Name _____

Notes _____

_____

_____

_____

_____

Vessel Name _____

Body of Water _____

Month _____ Official Number _____

Year _____ Gross Tonnage _____

Days Underway _____ Weather _____

Position Served _____ Fuel _____

Master Name _____

Notes _____

_____

_____

_____

_____

Trip Log

Vessel Name _____

Body of Water _____

Month _____ Official Number _____

Year _____ Gross Tonnage _____

Days Underway _____ Weather _____

Position Served _____ Fuel _____

Master Name _____

Notes _____

_____

_____

_____

_____

Vessel Name _____

Body of Water _____

Month _____ Official Number _____

Year _____ Gross Tonnage _____

Days Underway _____ Weather _____

Position Served _____ Fuel _____

Master Name _____

Notes _____

_____

_____

_____

_____

Trip Log

Vessel Name _____

Body of Water _____

Month _____ Official Number _____

Year _____ Gross Tonnage _____

Days Underway _____ Weather _____

Position Served _____ Fuel _____

Master Name _____

Notes _____

_____

_____

_____

_____

Vessel Name _____

Body of Water _____

Month _____ Official Number _____

Year _____ Gross Tonnage _____

Days Underway _____ Weather _____

Position Served _____ Fuel _____

Master Name _____

Notes _____

_____

_____

_____

_____

Trip Log

Vessel Name _____

Body of Water _____

Month _____ Official Number _____

Year _____ Gross Tonnage _____

Days Underway _____ Weather _____

Position Served _____ Fuel _____

Master Name _____

Notes _____

_____

_____

_____

_____

Vessel Name _____

Body of Water _____

Month _____ Official Number _____

Year _____ Gross Tonnage _____

Days Underway _____ Weather _____

Position Served _____ Fuel _____

Master Name _____

Notes _____

_____

_____

_____

_____

Trip Log

Vessel Name _____

Body of Water _____

Month _____   Official Number _____

Year _____   Gross Tonnage _____

Days Underway _____   Weather _____

Position Served _____   Fuel _____

Master Name _____

Notes _____

_____

_____

_____

_____

Vessel Name _____

Body of Water _____

Month _____   Official Number _____

Year _____   Gross Tonnage _____

Days Underway _____   Weather _____

Position Served _____   Fuel _____

Master Name _____

Notes _____

_____

_____

_____

_____

Trip Log

Vessel Name _____

Body of Water _____

Month _____ Official Number _____

Year _____ Gross Tonnage _____

Days Underway _____ Weather _____

Position Served _____ Fuel _____

Master Name _____

Notes _____

_____

_____

_____

_____

Vessel Name _____

Body of Water _____

Month _____ Official Number _____

Year _____ Gross Tonnage _____

Days Underway _____ Weather _____

Position Served _____ Fuel _____

Master Name _____

Notes _____

_____

_____

_____

_____

Trip Log

Vessel Name _____

Body of Water _____

Month _____ Official Number _____

Year _____ Gross Tonnage _____

Days Underway _____ Weather _____

Position Served _____ Fuel _____

Master Name _____

Notes _____

_____

_____

_____

_____

Vessel Name _____

Body of Water _____

Month _____ Official Number _____

Year _____ Gross Tonnage _____

Days Underway _____ Weather _____

Position Served _____ Fuel _____

Master Name _____

Notes _____

_____

_____

_____

_____

Trip Log

Vessel Name _____

Body of Water _____

Month _____ Official Number _____

Year _____ Gross Tonnage _____

Days Underway _____ Weather _____

Position Served _____ Fuel _____

Master Name _____

Notes _____

_____

_____

_____

_____

Vessel Name _____

Body of Water _____

Month _____ Official Number _____

Year _____ Gross Tonnage _____

Days Underway _____ Weather _____

Position Served _____ Fuel _____

Master Name _____

Notes _____

_____

_____

_____

_____

Trip Log

Vessel Name _____

Body of Water _____

Month _____   Official Number _____

Year _____   Gross Tonnage _____

Days Underway _____   Weather _____

Position Served _____   Fuel _____

Master Name _____

Notes _____

_____

_____

_____

_____

Vessel Name _____

Body of Water _____

Month _____   Official Number _____

Year _____   Gross Tonnage _____

Days Underway _____   Weather _____

Position Served _____   Fuel _____

Master Name _____

Notes _____

_____

_____

_____

_____

Journal

He makes me to lie down in green pastures; He leads me beside the still water. Psalm 23:2

Trip Log

Vessel Name _____

Body of Water _____

Month _____ Official Number _____

Year _____ Gross Tonnage _____

Days Underway _____ Weather _____

Position Served _____ Fuel _____

Master Name _____

Notes _____

_____

_____

_____

_____

Vessel Name _____

Body of Water _____

Month _____ Official Number _____

Year _____ Gross Tonnage _____

Days Underway _____ Weather _____

Position Served _____ Fuel _____

Master Name _____

Notes _____

_____

_____

_____

_____

Trip Log

Vessel Name _____

Body of Water _____

Month _____ Official Number _____

Year _____ Gross Tonnage _____

Days Underway _____ Weather _____

Position Served _____ Fuel _____

Master Name _____

Notes _____

_____

_____

_____

_____

Vessel Name _____

Body of Water _____

Month _____ Official Number _____

Year _____ Gross Tonnage _____

Days Underway _____ Weather _____

Position Served _____ Fuel _____

Master Name _____

Notes _____

_____

_____

_____

_____

Trip Log

Vessel Name _____

Body of Water _____

Month _____ Official Number _____

Year _____ Gross Tonnage _____

Days Underway _____ Weather _____

Position Served _____ Fuel _____

Master Name _____

Notes _____

_____

_____

_____

_____

Vessel Name _____

Body of Water _____

Month _____ Official Number _____

Year _____ Gross Tonnage _____

Days Underway _____ Weather _____

Position Served _____ Fuel _____

Master Name _____

Notes _____

_____

_____

_____

_____

Trip Log

Vessel Name _____

Body of Water _____

Month _____ Official Number _____

Year _____ Gross Tonnage _____

Days Underway _____ Weather _____

Position Served _____ Fuel _____

Master Name _____

Notes _____

_____

_____

_____

_____

Vessel Name _____

Body of Water _____

Month _____ Official Number _____

Year _____ Gross Tonnage _____

Days Underway _____ Weather _____

Position Served _____ Fuel _____

Master Name _____

Notes _____

_____

_____

_____

_____

Trip Log

Vessel Name _____

Body of Water _____

Month _____ Official Number _____

Year _____ Gross Tonnage _____

Days Underway _____ Weather _____

Position Served _____ Fuel _____

Master Name _____

Notes _____
_____
_____
_____
_____

Vessel Name _____

Body of Water _____

Month _____ Official Number _____

Year _____ Gross Tonnage _____

Days Underway _____ Weather _____

Position Served _____ Fuel _____

Master Name _____

Notes _____
_____
_____
_____
_____

Trip Log

Vessel Name _____

Body of Water _____

Month _____ Official Number _____

Year _____ Gross Tonnage _____

Days Underway _____ Weather _____

Position Served _____ Fuel _____

Master Name _____

Notes _____

_____

_____

_____

_____

Vessel Name _____

Body of Water _____

Month _____ Official Number _____

Year _____ Gross Tonnage _____

Days Underway _____ Weather _____

Position Served _____ Fuel _____

Master Name _____

Notes _____

_____

_____

_____

_____

Trip Log

Vessel Name _____

Body of Water _____

Month _____ Official Number _____

Year _____ Gross Tonnage _____

Days Underway _____ Weather _____

Position Served _____ Fuel _____

Master Name _____

Notes _____

_____

_____

_____

_____

Vessel Name _____

Body of Water _____

Month _____ Official Number _____

Year _____ Gross Tonnage _____

Days Underway _____ Weather _____

Position Served _____ Fuel _____

Master Name _____

Notes _____

_____

_____

_____

_____

Trip Log

Vessel Name _____

Body of Water _____

Month _____ Official Number _____

Year _____ Gross Tonnage _____

Days Underway _____ Weather _____

Position Served _____ Fuel _____

Master Name _____

Notes _____

_____

_____

_____

_____

Vessel Name _____

Body of Water _____

Month _____ Official Number _____

Year _____ Gross Tonnage _____

Days Underway _____ Weather _____

Position Served _____ Fuel _____

Master Name _____

Notes _____

_____

_____

_____

_____

Trip Log

Vessel Name _____

Body of Water _____

Month _____ Official Number _____

Year _____ Gross Tonnage _____

Days Underway _____ Weather _____

Position Served _____ Fuel _____

Master Name _____

Notes _____

_____

_____

_____

_____

Vessel Name _____

Body of Water _____

Month _____ Official Number _____

Year _____ Gross Tonnage _____

Days Underway _____ Weather _____

Position Served _____ Fuel _____

Master Name _____

Notes _____

_____

_____

_____

_____

Trip Log

Vessel Name _____

Body of Water _____

Month _____ Official Number _____

Year _____ Gross Tonnage _____

Days Underway _____ Weather _____

Position Served _____ Fuel _____

Master Name _____

Notes _____

_____

_____

_____

_____

Vessel Name _____

Body of Water _____

Month _____ Official Number _____

Year _____ Gross Tonnage _____

Days Underway _____ Weather _____

Position Served _____ Fuel _____

Master Name _____

Notes _____

_____

_____

_____

_____

Journal

_____
_____
_____
_____
_____
_____
_____
_____
_____
_____
_____
_____
_____
_____
_____
_____
_____
_____
_____
_____
_____
_____
_____
_____
_____
_____

We have this hope as an anchor for the soul, firm and secure.
Hebrews 6:19

Trip Log

Vessel Name _____

Body of Water _____

Month _____ Official Number _____

Year _____ Gross Tonnage _____

Days Underway _____ Weather _____

Position Served _____ Fuel _____

Master Name _____

Notes _____

_____

_____

_____

_____

Vessel Name _____

Body of Water _____

Month _____ Official Number _____

Year _____ Gross Tonnage _____

Days Underway _____ Weather _____

Position Served _____ Fuel _____

Master Name _____

Notes _____

_____

_____

_____

_____

Trip Log

Vessel Name _____

Body of Water _____

Month _____ Official Number _____

Year _____ Gross Tonnage _____

Days Underway _____ Weather _____

Position Served _____ Fuel _____

Master Name _____

Notes _____

_____

_____

_____

_____

Vessel Name _____

Body of Water _____

Month _____ Official Number _____

Year _____ Gross Tonnage _____

Days Underway _____ Weather _____

Position Served _____ Fuel _____

Master Name _____

Notes _____

_____

_____

_____

_____

Trip Log

Vessel Name _____

Body of Water _____

Month _____ Official Number _____

Year _____ Gross Tonnage _____

Days Underway _____ Weather _____

Position Served _____ Fuel _____

Master Name _____

Notes _____

_____

_____

_____

_____

Vessel Name _____

Body of Water _____

Month _____ Official Number _____

Year _____ Gross Tonnage _____

Days Underway _____ Weather _____

Position Served _____ Fuel _____

Master Name _____

Notes _____

_____

_____

_____

_____

Trip Log

Vessel Name _____

Body of Water _____

Month _____ Official Number _____

Year _____ Gross Tonnage _____

Days Underway _____ Weather _____

Position Served _____ Fuel _____

Master Name _____

Notes _____

_____

_____

_____

_____

Vessel Name _____

Body of Water _____

Month _____ Official Number _____

Year _____ Gross Tonnage _____

Days Underway _____ Weather _____

Position Served _____ Fuel _____

Master Name _____

Notes _____

_____

_____

_____

_____

Trip Log

Vessel Name _____

Body of Water _____

Month _____ Official Number _____

Year _____ Gross Tonnage _____

Days Underway _____ Weather _____

Position Served _____ Fuel _____

Master Name _____

Notes _____

_____

_____

_____

_____

Vessel Name _____

Body of Water _____

Month _____ Official Number _____

Year _____ Gross Tonnage _____

Days Underway _____ Weather _____

Position Served _____ Fuel _____

Master Name _____

Notes _____

_____

_____

_____

_____

Trip Log

Vessel Name _____

Body of Water _____

Month _____ Official Number _____

Year _____ Gross Tonnage _____

Days Underway _____ Weather _____

Position Served _____ Fuel _____

Master Name _____

Notes _____

_____

_____

_____

_____

Vessel Name _____

Body of Water _____

Month _____ Official Number _____

Year _____ Gross Tonnage _____

Days Underway _____ Weather _____

Position Served _____ Fuel _____

Master Name _____

Notes _____

_____

_____

_____

_____

Trip Log

Vessel Name _____

Body of Water _____

Month _____ Official Number _____

Year _____ Gross Tonnage _____

Days Underway _____ Weather _____

Position Served _____ Fuel _____

Master Name _____

Notes _____

_____

_____

_____

_____

Vessel Name _____

Body of Water _____

Month _____ Official Number _____

Year _____ Gross Tonnage _____

Days Underway _____ Weather _____

Position Served _____ Fuel _____

Master Name _____

Notes _____

_____

_____

_____

_____

Trip Log

Vessel Name _____

Body of Water _____

Month _____ Official Number _____

Year _____ Gross Tonnage _____

Days Underway _____ Weather _____

Position Served _____ Fuel _____

Master Name _____

Notes _____

_____

_____

_____

_____

Vessel Name _____

Body of Water _____

Month _____ Official Number _____

Year _____ Gross Tonnage _____

Days Underway _____ Weather _____

Position Served _____ Fuel _____

Master Name _____

Notes _____

_____

_____

_____

_____

Trip Log

Vessel Name _____

Body of Water _____

Month _____ Official Number _____

Year _____ Gross Tonnage _____

Days Underway _____ Weather _____

Position Served _____ Fuel _____

Master Name _____

Notes _____

_____

_____

_____

_____

Vessel Name _____

Body of Water _____

Month _____ Official Number _____

Year _____ Gross Tonnage _____

Days Underway _____ Weather _____

Position Served _____ Fuel _____

Master Name _____

Notes _____

_____

_____

_____

_____

Trip Log

Vessel Name _____

Body of Water _____

Month _____ Official Number _____

Year _____ Gross Tonnage _____

Days Underway _____ Weather _____

Position Served _____ Fuel _____

Master Name _____

Notes _____

_____

_____

_____

_____

Vessel Name _____

Body of Water _____

Month _____ Official Number _____

Year _____ Gross Tonnage _____

Days Underway _____ Weather _____

Position Served _____ Fuel _____

Master Name _____

Notes _____

_____

_____

_____

_____

Journal

_____
_____
_____
_____
_____
_____
_____
_____
_____
_____
_____
_____
_____
_____
_____
_____
_____
_____
_____
_____
_____
_____
_____
_____
_____
_____
_____
_____
_____

When you pass through the waters, I will be with you; And through the rivers, they shall not overflow you. Isaiah 43:2

Trip Log

Vessel Name _____

Body of Water _____

Month _____ Official Number _____

Year _____ Gross Tonnage _____

Days Underway _____ Weather _____

Position Served _____ Fuel _____

Master Name _____

Notes _____

_____

_____

_____

_____

Vessel Name _____

Body of Water _____

Month _____ Official Number _____

Year _____ Gross Tonnage _____

Days Underway _____ Weather _____

Position Served _____ Fuel _____

Master Name _____

Notes _____

_____

_____

_____

_____

Trip Log

Vessel Name _____

Body of Water _____

Month _____ Official Number _____

Year _____ Gross Tonnage _____

Days Underway _____ Weather _____

Position Served _____ Fuel _____

Master Name _____

Notes _____

_____

_____

_____

_____

Vessel Name _____

Body of Water _____

Month _____ Official Number _____

Year _____ Gross Tonnage _____

Days Underway _____ Weather _____

Position Served _____ Fuel _____

Master Name _____

Notes _____

_____

_____

_____

Trip Log

Vessel Name _____

Body of Water _____

Month _____ Official Number _____

Year _____ Gross Tonnage _____

Days Underway _____ Weather _____

Position Served _____ Fuel _____

Master Name _____

Notes

_____

_____

_____

_____

_____

Vessel Name _____

Body of Water _____

Month _____ Official Number _____

Year _____ Gross Tonnage _____

Days Underway _____ Weather _____

Position Served _____ Fuel _____

Master Name _____

Notes

_____

_____

_____

_____

_____

Trip Log

Vessel Name _____

Body of Water _____

Month _____ Official Number _____

Year _____ Gross Tonnage _____

Days Underway _____ Weather _____

Position Served _____ Fuel _____

Master Name _____

Notes _____

_____

_____

_____

_____

Vessel Name _____

Body of Water _____

Month _____ Official Number _____

Year _____ Gross Tonnage _____

Days Underway _____ Weather _____

Position Served _____ Fuel _____

Master Name _____

Notes _____

_____

_____

_____

_____

Trip Log

Vessel Name _____

Body of Water _____

Month _____ Official Number _____

Year _____ Gross Tonnage _____

Days Underway _____ Weather _____

Position Served _____ Fuel _____

Master Name _____

Notes _____

_____

_____

_____

_____

Vessel Name _____

Body of Water _____

Month _____ Official Number _____

Year _____ Gross Tonnage _____

Days Underway _____ Weather _____

Position Served _____ Fuel _____

Master Name _____

Notes _____

_____

_____

_____

_____

Trip Log

Vessel Name _____

Body of Water _____

Month _____ Official Number _____

Year _____ Gross Tonnage _____

Days Underway _____ Weather _____

Position Served _____ Fuel _____

Master Name _____

Notes _____

_____

_____

_____

_____

Vessel Name _____

Body of Water _____

Month _____ Official Number _____

Year _____ Gross Tonnage _____

Days Underway _____ Weather _____

Position Served _____ Fuel _____

Master Name _____

Notes _____

_____

_____

_____

_____

Trip Log

Vessel Name _____

Body of Water _____

Month _____ Official Number _____

Year _____ Gross Tonnage _____

Days Underway _____ Weather _____

Position Served _____ Fuel _____

Master Name _____

Notes _____

_____

_____

_____

_____

Vessel Name _____

Body of Water _____

Month _____ Official Number _____

Year _____ Gross Tonnage _____

Days Underway _____ Weather _____

Position Served _____ Fuel _____

Master Name _____

Notes _____

_____

_____

_____

_____

Trip Log

Vessel Name _____

Body of Water _____

Month _____ Official Number _____

Year _____ Gross Tonnage _____

Days Underway _____ Weather _____

Position Served _____ Fuel _____

Master Name _____

Notes _____

_____

_____

_____

_____

Vessel Name _____

Body of Water _____

Month _____ Official Number _____

Year _____ Gross Tonnage _____

Days Underway _____ Weather _____

Position Served _____ Fuel _____

Master Name _____

Notes _____

_____

_____

_____

Trip Log

Vessel Name _____

Body of Water _____

Month _____ Official Number _____

Year _____ Gross Tonnage _____

Days Underway _____ Weather _____

Position Served _____ Fuel _____

Master Name _____

Notes _____

_____

_____

_____

_____

Vessel Name _____

Body of Water _____

Month _____ Official Number _____

Year _____ Gross Tonnage _____

Days Underway _____ Weather _____

Position Served _____ Fuel _____

Master Name _____

Notes _____

_____

_____

_____

_____

Trip Log

Vessel Name _____

Body of Water _____

Month _____ Official Number _____

Year _____ Gross Tonnage _____

Days Underway _____ Weather _____

Position Served _____ Fuel _____

Master Name _____

Notes _____

_____

_____

_____

_____

Vessel Name _____

Body of Water _____

Month _____ Official Number _____

Year _____ Gross Tonnage _____

Days Underway _____ Weather _____

Position Served _____ Fuel _____

Master Name _____

Notes _____

_____

_____

_____

_____

Journal

Who can this be, that even the wind and sea obey Him? Mark 4:41

Trip Log

Vessel Name _____

Body of Water _____

Month _____ Official Number _____

Year _____ Gross Tonnage _____

Days Underway _____ Weather _____

Position Served _____ Fuel _____

Master Name _____

Notes _____

_____

_____

_____

_____

Vessel Name _____

Body of Water _____

Month _____ Official Number _____

Year _____ Gross Tonnage _____

Days Underway _____ Weather _____

Position Served _____ Fuel _____

Master Name _____

Notes _____

_____

_____

_____

_____

Trip Log

Vessel Name _____

Body of Water _____

Month _____ Official Number _____

Year _____ Gross Tonnage _____

Days Underway _____ Weather _____

Position Served _____ Fuel _____

Master Name _____

Notes _____

_____

_____

_____

_____

Vessel Name _____

Body of Water _____

Month _____ Official Number _____

Year _____ Gross Tonnage _____

Days Underway _____ Weather _____

Position Served _____ Fuel _____

Master Name _____

Notes _____

_____

_____

_____

_____

Trip Log

Vessel Name _____

Body of Water _____

Month _____ Official Number _____

Year _____ Gross Tonnage _____

Days Underway _____ Weather _____

Position Served _____ Fuel _____

Master Name _____

Notes _____

_____

_____

_____

_____

Vessel Name _____

Body of Water _____

Month _____ Official Number _____

Year _____ Gross Tonnage _____

Days Underway _____ Weather _____

Position Served _____ Fuel _____

Master Name _____

Notes _____

_____

_____

_____

_____

Trip Log

Vessel Name _____

Body of Water _____

Month _____ Official Number _____

Year _____ Gross Tonnage _____

Days Underway _____ Weather _____

Position Served _____ Fuel _____

Master Name _____

Notes _____

_____

_____

_____

_____

Vessel Name _____

Body of Water _____

Month _____ Official Number _____

Year _____ Gross Tonnage _____

Days Underway _____ Weather _____

Position Served _____ Fuel _____

Master Name _____

Notes _____

_____

_____

_____

_____

Trip Log

Vessel Name _____

Body of Water _____

Month _____ Official Number _____

Year _____ Gross Tonnage _____

Days Underway _____ Weather _____

Position Served _____ Fuel _____

Master Name _____

Notes _____

_____

_____

_____

_____

Vessel Name _____

Body of Water _____

Month _____ Official Number _____

Year _____ Gross Tonnage _____

Days Underway _____ Weather _____

Position Served _____ Fuel _____

Master Name _____

Notes _____

_____

_____

_____

_____

Trip Log

Vessel Name _____

Body of Water _____

Month _____ Official Number _____

Year _____ Gross Tonnage _____

Days Underway _____ Weather _____

Position Served _____ Fuel _____

Master Name _____

Notes _____

_____

_____

_____

_____

Vessel Name _____

Body of Water _____

Month _____ Official Number _____

Year _____ Gross Tonnage _____

Days Underway _____ Weather _____

Position Served _____ Fuel _____

Master Name _____

Notes _____

_____

_____

_____

_____

Trip Log

Vessel Name _____

Body of Water _____

Month _____ Official Number _____

Year _____ Gross Tonnage _____

Days Underway _____ Weather _____

Position Served _____ Fuel _____

Master Name _____

Notes _____

_____

_____

_____

_____

_____

Vessel Name _____

Body of Water _____

Month _____ Official Number _____

Year _____ Gross Tonnage _____

Days Underway _____ Weather _____

Position Served _____ Fuel _____

Master Name _____

Notes _____

_____

_____

_____

_____

Trip Log

Vessel Name _____

Body of Water _____

Month _____ Official Number _____

Year _____ Gross Tonnage _____

Days Underway _____ Weather _____

Position Served _____ Fuel _____

Master Name _____

Notes _____

_____

_____

_____

_____

Vessel Name _____

Body of Water _____

Month _____ Official Number _____

Year _____ Gross Tonnage _____

Days Underway _____ Weather _____

Position Served _____ Fuel _____

Master Name _____

Notes _____

_____

_____

_____

_____

Trip Log

Vessel Name _____

Body of Water _____

Month _____ Official Number _____

Year _____ Gross Tonnage _____

Days Underway _____ Weather _____

Position Served _____ Fuel _____

Master Name _____

Notes _____

_____

_____

_____

_____

Vessel Name _____

Body of Water _____

Month _____ Official Number _____

Year _____ Gross Tonnage _____

Days Underway _____ Weather _____

Position Served _____ Fuel _____

Master Name _____

Notes _____

_____

_____

_____

_____

Trip Log

Vessel Name _____

Body of Water _____

Month _____ Official Number _____

Year _____ Gross Tonnage _____

Days Underway _____ Weather _____

Position Served _____ Fuel _____

Master Name _____

Notes

_____

_____

_____

_____

_____

Vessel Name _____

Body of Water _____

Month _____ Official Number _____

Year _____ Gross Tonnage _____

Days Underway _____ Weather _____

Position Served _____ Fuel _____

Master Name _____

Notes

_____

_____

_____

_____

_____

Journal

_____
_____
_____
_____
_____
_____
_____
_____
_____
_____
_____
_____
_____
_____
_____
_____
_____
_____
_____
_____
_____
_____
_____
_____
_____
_____
_____
_____

With joy you will draw water from the wells of salvation.   Isaiah 12:3

Trip Log

Vessel Name _____

Body of Water _____

Month _____ Official Number _____

Year _____ Gross Tonnage _____

Days Underway _____ Weather _____

Position Served _____ Fuel _____

Master Name _____

Notes _____
_____
_____
_____
_____

Vessel Name _____

Body of Water _____

Month _____ Official Number _____

Year _____ Gross Tonnage _____

Days Underway _____ Weather _____

Position Served _____ Fuel _____

Master Name _____

Notes _____
_____
_____
_____
_____

Trip Log

Vessel Name _____

Body of Water _____

Month _____ Official Number _____

Year _____ Gross Tonnage _____

Days Underway _____ Weather _____

Position Served _____ Fuel _____

Master Name _____

Notes

_____

_____

_____

_____

_____

Vessel Name _____

Body of Water _____

Month _____ Official Number _____

Year _____ Gross Tonnage _____

Days Underway _____ Weather _____

Position Served _____ Fuel _____

Master Name _____

Notes

_____

_____

_____

_____

_____

Trip Log

Vessel Name _____

Body of Water _____

Month _____ Official Number _____

Year _____ Gross Tonnage _____

Days Underway _____ Weather _____

Position Served _____ Fuel _____

Master Name _____

Notes _____

_____

_____

_____

_____

Vessel Name _____

Body of Water _____

Month _____ Official Number _____

Year _____ Gross Tonnage _____

Days Underway _____ Weather _____

Position Served _____ Fuel _____

Master Name _____

Notes _____

_____

_____

_____

_____

Trip Log

Vessel Name _____

Body of Water _____

Month _____ Official Number _____

Year _____ Gross Tonnage _____

Days Underway _____ Weather _____

Position Served _____ Fuel _____

Master Name _____

Notes _____

_____

_____

_____

_____

Vessel Name _____

Body of Water _____

Month _____ Official Number _____

Year _____ Gross Tonnage _____

Days Underway _____ Weather _____

Position Served _____ Fuel _____

Master Name _____

Notes _____

_____

_____

_____

_____

Trip Log

Vessel Name _____

Body of Water _____

Month _____ Official Number _____

Year _____ Gross Tonnage _____

Days Underway _____ Weather _____

Position Served _____ Fuel _____

Master Name _____

Notes _____

_____

_____

_____

_____

Vessel Name _____

Body of Water _____

Month _____ Official Number _____

Year _____ Gross Tonnage _____

Days Underway _____ Weather _____

Position Served _____ Fuel _____

Master Name _____

Notes _____

_____

_____

_____

_____

Trip Log

Vessel Name _____

Body of Water _____

Month _____ Official Number _____

Year _____ Gross Tonnage _____

Days Underway _____ Weather _____

Position Served _____ Fuel _____

Master Name _____

Notes _____

_____

_____

_____

_____

Vessel Name _____

Body of Water _____

Month _____ Official Number _____

Year _____ Gross Tonnage _____

Days Underway _____ Weather _____

Position Served _____ Fuel _____

Master Name _____

Notes _____

_____

_____

_____

Trip Log

Vessel Name _____

Body of Water _____

Month _____ Official Number _____

Year _____ Gross Tonnage _____

Days Underway _____ Weather _____

Position Served _____ Fuel _____

Master Name _____

Notes _____

_____

_____

_____

_____

Vessel Name _____

Body of Water _____

Month _____ Official Number _____

Year _____ Gross Tonnage _____

Days Underway _____ Weather _____

Position Served _____ Fuel _____

Master Name _____

Notes _____

_____

_____

_____

Trip Log

Vessel Name _____
Body of Water _____
Month _____ Official Number _____
Year _____ Gross Tonnage _____
Days Underway _____ Weather _____
Position Served _____ Fuel _____
Master Name _____

Notes _____
_____
_____
_____
_____

Vessel Name _____
Body of Water _____
Month _____ Official Number _____
Year _____ Gross Tonnage _____
Days Underway _____ Weather _____
Position Served _____ Fuel _____
Master Name _____

Notes _____
_____
_____
_____

Trip Log

Vessel Name _____

Body of Water _____

Month _____ Official Number _____

Year _____ Gross Tonnage _____

Days Underway _____ Weather _____

Position Served _____ Fuel _____

Master Name _____

Notes _____

_____

_____

_____

_____

Vessel Name _____

Body of Water _____

Month _____ Official Number _____

Year _____ Gross Tonnage _____

Days Underway _____ Weather _____

Position Served _____ Fuel _____

Master Name _____

Notes _____

_____

_____

_____

_____

Trip Log

Vessel Name _____

Body of Water _____

Month _____ Official Number _____

Year _____ Gross Tonnage _____

Days Underway _____ Weather _____

Position Served _____ Fuel _____

Master Name _____

Notes _____

_____

_____

_____

_____

Vessel Name _____

Body of Water _____

Month _____ Official Number _____

Year _____ Gross Tonnage _____

Days Underway _____ Weather _____

Position Served _____ Fuel _____

Master Name _____

Notes _____

_____

_____

_____

_____

Journal

_____

_____

_____

_____

_____

_____

_____

_____

_____

_____

_____

_____

_____

_____

_____

_____

_____

_____

_____

_____

_____

_____

_____

_____

_____

"Come follow me," Jesus said, "and I will make you fishers of men."
Matthew 4:19

Trip Log

Vessel Name _____

Body of Water _____

Month _____ Official Number _____

Year _____ Gross Tonnage _____

Days Underway _____ Weather _____

Position Served _____ Fuel _____

Master Name _____

Notes _____

_____

_____

_____

_____

Vessel Name _____

Body of Water _____

Month _____ Official Number _____

Year _____ Gross Tonnage _____

Days Underway _____ Weather _____

Position Served _____ Fuel _____

Master Name _____

Notes _____

_____

_____

_____

_____

Trip Log

Vessel Name _____

Body of Water _____

Month _____ Official Number _____

Year _____ Gross Tonnage _____

Days Underway _____ Weather _____

Position Served _____ Fuel _____

Master Name _____

Notes _____

_____

_____

_____

_____

Vessel Name _____

Body of Water _____

Month _____ Official Number _____

Year _____ Gross Tonnage _____

Days Underway _____ Weather _____

Position Served _____ Fuel _____

Master Name _____

Notes _____

_____

_____

_____

_____

Trip Log

Vessel Name _____

Body of Water _____

Month _____ Official Number _____

Year _____ Gross Tonnage _____

Days Underway _____ Weather _____

Position Served _____ Fuel _____

Master Name _____

Notes _____
_____
_____
_____
_____

Vessel Name _____

Body of Water _____

Month _____ Official Number _____

Year _____ Gross Tonnage _____

Days Underway _____ Weather _____

Position Served _____ Fuel _____

Master Name _____

Notes _____
_____
_____
_____
_____

Trip Log

Vessel Name _____

Body of Water _____

Month _____ Official Number _____

Year _____ Gross Tonnage _____

Days Underway _____ Weather _____

Position Served _____ Fuel _____

Master Name _____

Notes _____

_____

_____

_____

_____

Vessel Name _____

Body of Water _____

Month _____ Official Number _____

Year _____ Gross Tonnage _____

Days Underway _____ Weather _____

Position Served _____ Fuel _____

Master Name _____

Notes _____

_____

_____

_____

_____

Trip Log

Vessel Name _____

Body of Water _____

Month _____ Official Number _____

Year _____ Gross Tonnage _____

Days Underway _____ Weather _____

Position Served _____ Fuel _____

Master Name _____

Notes _____

_____

_____

_____

_____

Vessel Name _____

Body of Water _____

Month _____ Official Number _____

Year _____ Gross Tonnage _____

Days Underway _____ Weather _____

Position Served _____ Fuel _____

Master Name _____

Notes _____

_____

_____

_____

_____

Trip Log

Vessel Name _____

Body of Water _____

Month _____ Official Number _____

Year _____ Gross Tonnage _____

Days Underway _____ Weather _____

Position Served _____ Fuel _____

Master Name _____

Notes _____

_____

_____

_____

_____

Vessel Name _____

Body of Water _____

Month _____ Official Number _____

Year _____ Gross Tonnage _____

Days Underway _____ Weather _____

Position Served _____ Fuel _____

Master Name _____

Notes _____

_____

_____

_____

_____

Trip Log

Vessel Name _____

Body of Water _____

Month _____ Official Number _____

Year _____ Gross Tonnage _____

Days Underway _____ Weather _____

Position Served _____ Fuel _____

Master Name _____

Notes _____

_____

_____

_____

_____

Vessel Name _____

Body of Water _____

Month _____ Official Number _____

Year _____ Gross Tonnage _____

Days Underway _____ Weather _____

Position Served _____ Fuel _____

Master Name _____

Notes _____

_____

_____

_____

_____

Trip Log

Vessel Name _____

Body of Water _____

Month _____ Official Number _____

Year _____ Gross Tonnage _____

Days Underway _____ Weather _____

Position Served _____ Fuel _____

Master Name _____

Notes _____

_____

_____

_____

_____

Vessel Name _____

Body of Water _____

Month _____ Official Number _____

Year _____ Gross Tonnage _____

Days Underway _____ Weather _____

Position Served _____ Fuel _____

Master Name _____

Notes _____

_____

_____

_____

_____

Trip Log

Vessel Name _____

Body of Water _____

Month _____ Official Number _____

Year _____ Gross Tonnage _____

Days Underway _____ Weather _____

Position Served _____ Fuel _____

Master Name _____

Notes _____

_____

_____

_____

_____

Vessel Name _____

Body of Water _____

Month _____ Official Number _____

Year _____ Gross Tonnage _____

Days Underway _____ Weather _____

Position Served _____ Fuel _____

Master Name _____

Notes _____

_____

_____

_____

_____

Trip Log

Vessel Name _____

Body of Water _____

Month _____ Official Number _____

Year _____ Gross Tonnage _____

Days Underway _____ Weather _____

Position Served _____ Fuel _____

Master Name _____

Notes _____

_____

_____

_____

_____

Vessel Name _____

Body of Water _____

Month _____ Official Number _____

Year _____ Gross Tonnage _____

Days Underway _____ Weather _____

Position Served _____ Fuel _____

Master Name _____

Notes _____

_____

_____

_____

_____

Journal

And when they brought their boats to land, they left everything and followed Him. Luke 5:11

Trip Log

Vessel Name _____

Body of Water _____

Month _____ Official Number _____

Year _____ Gross Tonnage _____

Days Underway _____ Weather _____

Position Served _____ Fuel _____

Master Name _____

Notes _____

_____

_____

_____

_____

Vessel Name _____

Body of Water _____

Month _____ Official Number _____

Year _____ Gross Tonnage _____

Days Underway _____ Weather _____

Position Served _____ Fuel _____

Master Name _____

Notes _____

_____

_____

_____

_____

Trip Log

Vessel Name _____

Body of Water _____

Month _____ Official Number _____

Year _____ Gross Tonnage _____

Days Underway _____ Weather _____

Position Served _____ Fuel _____

Master Name _____

Notes _____
_____
_____
_____
_____

Vessel Name _____

Body of Water _____

Month _____ Official Number _____

Year _____ Gross Tonnage _____

Days Underway _____ Weather _____

Position Served _____ Fuel _____

Master Name _____

Notes _____
_____
_____
_____

Trip Log

Vessel Name _____

Body of Water _____

Month _____ Official Number _____

Year _____ Gross Tonnage _____

Days Underway _____ Weather _____

Position Served _____ Fuel _____

Master Name _____

Notes _____

_____

_____

_____

_____

Vessel Name _____

Body of Water _____

Month _____ Official Number _____

Year _____ Gross Tonnage _____

Days Underway _____ Weather _____

Position Served _____ Fuel _____

Master Name _____

Notes _____

_____

_____

_____

Trip Log

Vessel Name _____

Body of Water _____

Month _____ Official Number _____

Year _____ Gross Tonnage _____

Days Underway _____ Weather _____

Position Served _____ Fuel _____

Master Name _____

Notes _____

_____

_____

_____

_____

Vessel Name _____

Body of Water _____

Month _____ Official Number _____

Year _____ Gross Tonnage _____

Days Underway _____ Weather _____

Position Served _____ Fuel _____

Master Name _____

Notes _____

_____

_____

_____

_____

Trip Log

Vessel Name _____

Body of Water _____

Month _____ Official Number _____

Year _____ Gross Tonnage _____

Days Underway _____ Weather _____

Position Served _____ Fuel _____

Master Name _____

Notes _____

_____

_____

_____

_____

Vessel Name _____

Body of Water _____

Month _____ Official Number _____

Year _____ Gross Tonnage _____

Days Underway _____ Weather _____

Position Served _____ Fuel _____

Master Name _____

Notes _____

_____

_____

_____

_____

Trip Log

Vessel Name _____

Body of Water _____

Month _____ Official Number _____

Year _____ Gross Tonnage _____

Days Underway _____ Weather _____

Position Served _____ Fuel _____

Master Name _____

Notes _____

_____

_____

_____

_____

Vessel Name _____

Body of Water _____

Month _____ Official Number _____

Year _____ Gross Tonnage _____

Days Underway _____ Weather _____

Position Served _____ Fuel _____

Master Name _____

Notes _____

_____

_____

_____

_____

Trip Log

Vessel Name _____

Body of Water _____

Month _____ Official Number _____

Year _____ Gross Tonnage _____

Days Underway _____ Weather _____

Position Served _____ Fuel _____

Master Name _____

Notes _____

_____

_____

_____

_____

Vessel Name _____

Body of Water _____

Month _____ Official Number _____

Year _____ Gross Tonnage _____

Days Underway _____ Weather _____

Position Served _____ Fuel _____

Master Name _____

Notes _____

_____

_____

_____

Trip Log

Vessel Name _____

Body of Water _____

Month _____ Official Number _____

Year _____ Gross Tonnage _____

Days Underway _____ Weather _____

Position Served _____ Fuel _____

Master Name _____

Notes _____

_____

_____

_____

_____

_____

Vessel Name _____

Body of Water _____

Month _____ Official Number _____

Year _____ Gross Tonnage _____

Days Underway _____ Weather _____

Position Served _____ Fuel _____

Master Name _____

Notes _____

_____

_____

_____

_____

Trip Log

Vessel Name _____

Body of Water _____

Month _____ Official Number _____

Year _____ Gross Tonnage _____

Days Underway _____ Weather _____

Position Served _____ Fuel _____

Master Name _____

Notes _____

_____

_____

_____

_____

Vessel Name _____

Body of Water _____

Month _____ Official Number _____

Year _____ Gross Tonnage _____

Days Underway _____ Weather _____

Position Served _____ Fuel _____

Master Name _____

Notes _____

_____

_____

_____

Trip Log

Vessel Name _____

Body of Water _____

Month _____ Official Number _____

Year _____ Gross Tonnage _____

Days Underway _____ Weather _____

Position Served _____ Fuel _____

Master Name _____

Notes _____

_____

_____

_____

_____

Vessel Name _____

Body of Water _____

Month _____ Official Number _____

Year _____ Gross Tonnage _____

Days Underway _____ Weather _____

Position Served _____ Fuel _____

Master Name _____

Notes _____

_____

_____

_____

_____

Journal

Mightier than the waves of the sea is His love for you. Psalm 95:4

Trip Log

Vessel Name _____
Body of Water _____
Month _____   Official Number _____
Year _____   Gross Tonnage _____
Days Underway _____   Weather _____
Position Served _____   Fuel _____
Master Name _____

Notes _____
_____
_____
_____
_____

Vessel Name _____
Body of Water _____
Month _____   Official Number _____
Year _____   Gross Tonnage _____
Days Underway _____   Weather _____
Position Served _____   Fuel _____
Master Name _____

Notes _____
_____
_____
_____

Trip Log

Vessel Name _____

Body of Water _____

Month _____ Official Number _____

Year _____ Gross Tonnage _____

Days Underway _____ Weather _____

Position Served _____ Fuel _____

Master Name _____

Notes

_____

_____

_____

_____

_____

Vessel Name _____

Body of Water _____

Month _____ Official Number _____

Year _____ Gross Tonnage _____

Days Underway _____ Weather _____

Position Served _____ Fuel _____

Master Name _____

Notes

_____

_____

_____

_____

_____

Trip Log

Vessel Name _____

Body of Water _____

Month _____ Official Number _____

Year _____ Gross Tonnage _____

Days Underway _____ Weather _____

Position Served _____ Fuel _____

Master Name _____

Notes
_____

_____

_____

_____

_____

Vessel Name _____

Body of Water _____

Month _____ Official Number _____

Year _____ Gross Tonnage _____

Days Underway _____ Weather _____

Position Served _____ Fuel _____

Master Name _____

Notes
_____

_____

_____

_____

_____

Trip Log

Vessel Name _____

Body of Water _____

Month _____ Official Number _____

Year _____ Gross Tonnage _____

Days Underway _____ Weather _____

Position Served _____ Fuel _____

Master Name _____

Notes _____

_____

_____

_____

_____

Vessel Name _____

Body of Water _____

Month _____ Official Number _____

Year _____ Gross Tonnage _____

Days Underway _____ Weather _____

Position Served _____ Fuel _____

Master Name _____

Notes _____

_____

_____

_____

Trip Log

Vessel Name _____

Body of Water _____

Month _____ Official Number _____

Year _____ Gross Tonnage _____

Days Underway _____ Weather _____

Position Served _____ Fuel _____

Master Name _____

Notes _____

_____

_____

_____

_____

Vessel Name _____

Body of Water _____

Month _____ Official Number _____

Year _____ Gross Tonnage _____

Days Underway _____ Weather _____

Position Served _____ Fuel _____

Master Name _____

Notes _____

_____

_____

_____

_____

Trip Log

Vessel Name _____

Body of Water _____

Month _____ Official Number _____

Year _____ Gross Tonnage _____

Days Underway _____ Weather _____

Position Served _____ Fuel _____

Master Name _____

Notes _____

_____

_____

_____

_____

Vessel Name _____

Body of Water _____

Month _____ Official Number _____

Year _____ Gross Tonnage _____

Days Underway _____ Weather _____

Position Served _____ Fuel _____

Master Name _____

Notes _____

_____

_____

_____

_____

Trip Log

Vessel Name _____

Body of Water _____

Month _____ Official Number _____

Year _____ Gross Tonnage _____

Days Underway _____ Weather _____

Position Served _____ Fuel _____

Master Name _____

Notes

_____

_____

_____

_____

_____

Vessel Name _____

Body of Water _____

Month _____ Official Number _____

Year _____ Gross Tonnage _____

Days Underway _____ Weather _____

Position Served _____ Fuel _____

Master Name _____

Notes

_____

_____

_____

_____

_____

Trip Log

Vessel Name _____

Body of Water _____

Month _____ Official Number _____

Year _____ Gross Tonnage _____

Days Underway _____ Weather _____

Position Served _____ Fuel _____

Master Name _____

Notes _____

_____

_____

_____

_____

Vessel Name _____

Body of Water _____

Month _____ Official Number _____

Year _____ Gross Tonnage _____

Days Underway _____ Weather _____

Position Served _____ Fuel _____

Master Name _____

Notes _____

_____

_____

_____

_____

Trip Log

Vessel Name _____

Body of Water _____

Month _____ Official Number _____

Year _____ Gross Tonnage _____

Days Underway _____ Weather _____

Position Served _____ Fuel _____

Master Name _____

Notes _____

_____

_____

_____

_____

Vessel Name _____

Body of Water _____

Month _____ Official Number _____

Year _____ Gross Tonnage _____

Days Underway _____ Weather _____

Position Served _____ Fuel _____

Master Name _____

Notes _____

_____

_____

_____

_____

Trip Log

Vessel Name _____

Body of Water _____

Month _____ Official Number _____

Year _____ Gross Tonnage _____

Days Underway _____ Weather _____

Position Served _____ Fuel _____

Master Name _____

Notes _____

_____

_____

_____

_____

Vessel Name _____

Body of Water _____

Month _____ Official Number _____

Year _____ Gross Tonnage _____

Days Underway _____ Weather _____

Position Served _____ Fuel _____

Master Name _____

Notes _____

_____

_____

_____

Journal

_____
_____
_____
_____
_____
_____
_____
_____
_____
_____
_____
_____
_____
_____
_____
_____
_____
_____
_____
_____
_____
_____
_____

More than the sounds of many waters, than the mighty breakers of the
sea, the Lord on high is mighty. Psalm 93:4

Trip Log

Vessel Name _____
Body of Water _____
Month _____ Official Number _____
Year _____ Gross Tonnage _____
Days Underway _____ Weather _____
Position Served _____ Fuel _____
Master Name _____

Notes _____

_____

_____

_____

_____

Vessel Name _____
Body of Water _____
Month _____ Official Number _____
Year _____ Gross Tonnage _____
Days Underway _____ Weather _____
Position Served _____ Fuel _____
Master Name _____

Notes _____

_____

_____

_____

_____

Trip Log

Vessel Name _____

Body of Water _____

Month _____ Official Number _____

Year _____ Gross Tonnage _____

Days Underway _____ Weather _____

Position Served _____ Fuel _____

Master Name _____

Notes _____

_____

_____

_____

_____

Vessel Name _____

Body of Water _____

Month _____ Official Number _____

Year _____ Gross Tonnage _____

Days Underway _____ Weather _____

Position Served _____ Fuel _____

Master Name _____

Notes _____

_____

_____

_____

Trip Log

Vessel Name _____

Body of Water _____

Month _____ Official Number _____

Year _____ Gross Tonnage _____

Days Underway _____ Weather _____

Position Served _____ Fuel _____

Master Name _____

Notes _____

_____

_____

_____

_____

Vessel Name _____

Body of Water _____

Month _____ Official Number _____

Year _____ Gross Tonnage _____

Days Underway _____ Weather _____

Position Served _____ Fuel _____

Master Name _____

Notes _____

_____

_____

_____

_____

Trip Log

Vessel Name _____

Body of Water _____

Month _____ Official Number _____

Year _____ Gross Tonnage _____

Days Underway _____ Weather _____

Position Served _____ Fuel _____

Master Name _____

Notes _____

_____

_____

_____

_____

Vessel Name _____

Body of Water _____

Month _____ Official Number _____

Year _____ Gross Tonnage _____

Days Underway _____ Weather _____

Position Served _____ Fuel _____

Master Name _____

Notes _____

_____

_____

_____

_____

Trip Log

Vessel Name _____

Body of Water _____

Month _____ Official Number _____

Year _____ Gross Tonnage _____

Days Underway _____ Weather _____

Position Served _____ Fuel _____

Master Name _____

Notes _____

_____

_____

_____

_____

Vessel Name _____

Body of Water _____

Month _____ Official Number _____

Year _____ Gross Tonnage _____

Days Underway _____ Weather _____

Position Served _____ Fuel _____

Master Name _____

Notes _____

_____

_____

_____

_____

Trip Log

Vessel Name _____

Body of Water _____

Month _____ Official Number _____

Year _____ Gross Tonnage _____

Days Underway _____ Weather _____

Position Served _____ Fuel _____

Master Name _____

Notes _____

_____

_____

_____

_____

Vessel Name _____

Body of Water _____

Month _____ Official Number _____

Year _____ Gross Tonnage _____

Days Underway _____ Weather _____

Position Served _____ Fuel _____

Master Name _____

Notes _____

_____

_____

_____

_____

Trip Log

Vessel Name _____

Body of Water _____

Month _____ Official Number _____

Year _____ Gross Tonnage _____

Days Underway _____ Weather _____

Position Served _____ Fuel _____

Master Name _____

Notes
_____

_____

_____

_____

_____

Vessel Name _____

Body of Water _____

Month _____ Official Number _____

Year _____ Gross Tonnage _____

Days Underway _____ Weather _____

Position Served _____ Fuel _____

Master Name _____

Notes
_____

_____

_____

_____

_____

Trip Log

Vessel Name _____

Body of Water _____

Month _____ Official Number _____

Year _____ Gross Tonnage _____

Days Underway _____ Weather _____

Position Served _____ Fuel _____

Master Name _____

Notes _____

_____

_____

_____

_____

Vessel Name _____

Body of Water _____

Month _____ Official Number _____

Year _____ Gross Tonnage _____

Days Underway _____ Weather _____

Position Served _____ Fuel _____

Master Name _____

Notes _____

_____

_____

_____

Journal

And He said to me, "It is done! I am the Alpha and the Omega, the Beginning and the End. I will give of the fountain of the water of life freely to him who thirsts." Revelation 21:6

Conclusion

Congratulations on completing Don't Rock the Boat!

I sincerely hope you found the content useful!

I put countless hours into the creation of this book and making my readers satisfied is my number one priority!

If you enjoyed this book, please take a few minutes out of your day to leave a positive review for it on Amazon, it would mean the WORLD to me!

Again, thanks for purchasing my book!

Captain Jack

Made in the USA
Monee, IL
31 October 2021